MOUSE DEER

By Colleen Sexton

Minneapolis, Minnesota

Credits:

Cover and title page, © Matt Tilghman/Shutterstock, © teimy_photos/Shutterstock, and © Rungratchanee Pimathai/Shutterstock; 3, © Bernard Bialorucki/iStock; 4–5, © blickwinkel/McPHOTO/WAS/Alamy; 6–7, © Biggy TLC/Shutterstock; 8–9, © BirdHunter591/iStock; 10, © de2marco/Shutterstock; 11, © Chrissi4788/Shutterstock; 13, © Nuwat Phansuwan/Shutterstock; 14–15, © [@] Sound/iStock; 17, © PhotocechCZ/Shutterstock; 18–19, © dinukask/Shutterstock; 20–21, © blickwinkel/Layer/Alamy; 22, © cammep/Shutterstock; and 23, © sittitap/Shutterstock.

Bearport Publishing Company Product Development Team
President: Jen Jenson; Director of Product Development: Spencer Brinker; Senior Editor: Allison Juda; Editor: Charly Haley; Associate Editor: Naomi Reich; Senior Designer: Colin O'Dea; Associate Designer: Elena Klinkner; Product Development Assistant: Anita Stasson

Library of Congress Cataloging-in-Publication Data

Names: Sexton, Colleen A., 1967- author.
Title: Mouse deer / Colleen Sexton.
Description: Minneapolis, Minnesota : Bearport Publishing Company, [2023] | Series: Library of awesome animals | Includes bibliographical references and index.
Identifiers: LCCN 2022006992 (print) | LCCN 2022006993 (ebook) | ISBN 9798885091107 (library binding) | ISBN 9798885091176 (paperback) | ISBN 9798885091244 (ebook)
Subjects: LCSH: Chevrotains--Juvenile literature.
Classification: LCC QL737.U595 S49 2023 (print) | LCC QL737.U595 (ebook) | DDC 599.63--dc23/eng/20220304
LC record available at https://lccn.loc.gov/2022006992
LC ebook record available at https://lccn.loc.gov/2022006993

Copyright © 2023 Bearport Publishing Company. All rights reserved. No part of this publication may be reproduced in whole or in part, stored in any retrieval system, or transmitted in any form or by any means, electronic, mechanical, photocopying, recording, or otherwise, without written permission from the publisher.

For more information, write to Bearport Publishing, 5357 Penn Avenue South, Minneapolis, MN 55419. Printed in the United States of America.

Contents

Awesome Mouse Deer! 4
From Head to Hooves 6
Found in Forests 8
What's On the Menu? 10
Make Your Mark 12
Quiet Creatures 14
Danger! 16
A Little Baby 18
Growing Up 20

Information Station 22
Glossary 23
Index 24
Read More 24
Learn More Online 24
About the Author 24

AWESOME
Mouse Deer!

A mouse deer is sleeping when suddenly its round ears perk up. **TWITCH!** The little animal opens its big eyes. It rises on skinny legs and starts sprinting between trees. Whether resting quietly or running quickly, mouse deer are awesome!

MOUSE DEER ARE ALSO CALLED CHEVROTAINS (SHEV-RUH-TAYNS). THIS NAME MEANS LITTLE GOAT IN FRENCH.

5

From Head to Hooves

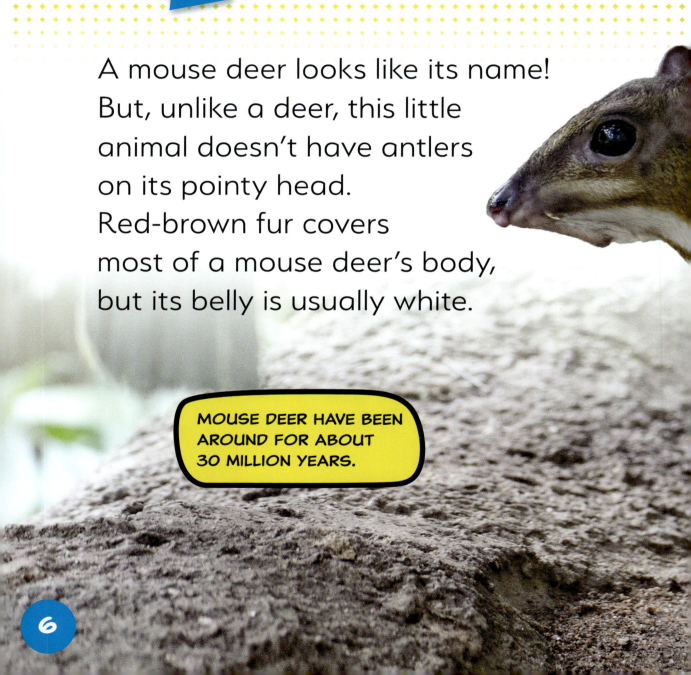

A mouse deer looks like its name! But, unlike a deer, this little animal doesn't have antlers on its pointy head. Red-brown fur covers most of a mouse deer's body, but its belly is usually white.

MOUSE DEER HAVE BEEN AROUND FOR ABOUT 30 MILLION YEARS.

A mouse deer can have white spots or stripes, too. **Hooves** on the ends of its tiny feet help the animal step through the forest.

Found in Forests

There are 10 kinds of mouse deer living in southeast Asia and parts of Africa. They make their homes where the forest is thick with trees and plants. The little animals stay near water, too.

What's On the Menu?

Mouse deer have plenty to eat in their forest homes. They mostly nibble on plants, including leaves, buds, and grasses. The animals search for fruit that has fallen on the ground, and they may even eat underwater plants. Some kinds of mouse deer gobble up insects or other tiny animals, too. **MUNCH!**

MOUSE DEER EAT AT NIGHT. THEY SPEND THEIR DAYS RESTING AND SLEEPING.

Make Your Mark

Most mouse deer live alone in their own **territory**. They tell other mouse deer to stay away. How? The animals mark their areas with poop and pee! **PEE-YEW!**

Sometimes, mouse deer fight over territory. **Males** bite each other with their sharp **tusks**. Luckily, thick skin on their bodies **protects** the animals during these fights.

> SOME MOUSE DEER RUB THEIR CHINS OVER BRANCHES AND TREE ROOTS TO MARK THEIR TERRITORY, TOO.

Quiet Creatures

When they aren't feeding or fighting over territory, mouse deer hide. These quiet creatures are easily frightened. They jump away quickly at the smallest sounds.

Mouse deer silently slip between trees when they roam the forest. Being quiet and hiding helps mouse deer stay safe from other animals.

Danger!

Even though mouse deer hide, sometimes **predators** still find them. Owls and hawks might attack from above. On the ground, snakes, tigers, and leopards are ready to pounce. Mouse deer cry out when they sense danger. They sometimes stomp the ground with their hooves. **THUMP, THUMP!** The little deer escape danger by running in a zigzag pattern or jumping into water.

> PEOPLE ARE A DANGER, TOO. THEY HUNT MOUSE DEER AND HARM FORESTS WHERE THE ANIMALS LIVE.

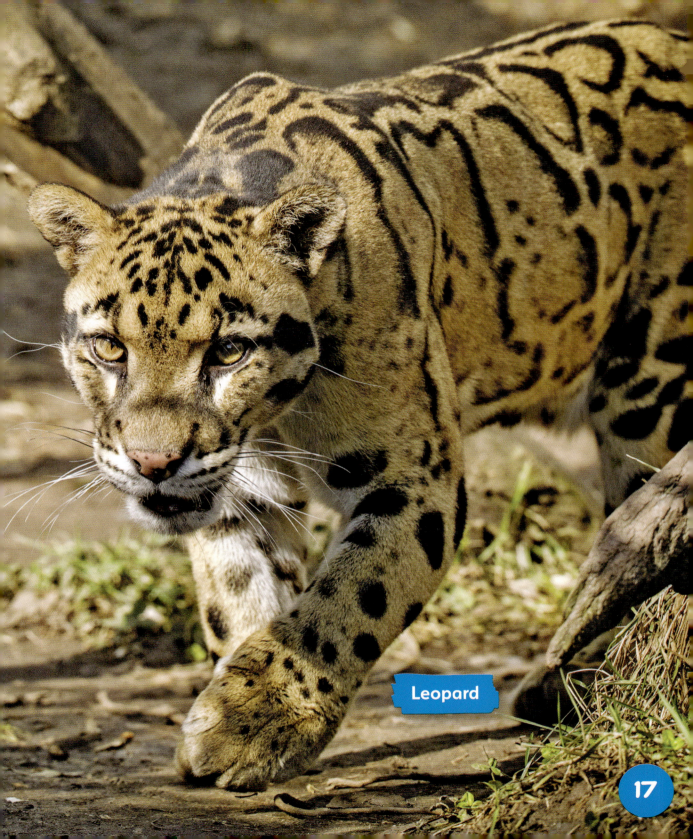

Leopard

17

A Little Baby

While most mouse deer live alone, they do come together to **mate**. Four to nine months after mating, a **female** mouse deer gives birth to a baby. The mother hides her little **fawn** in the forest to keep it safe.

MOUSE DEER FAWNS CAN STAND WITHIN AN HOUR AFTER THEY ARE BORN.

But the mother doesn't spend much time with her new baby. She leaves the fawn alone and returns only to feed it.

Growing Up

The newborn fawn drinks milk from its mother's body. In a few weeks, the baby can eat leaves and grasses, too. After three to six months, the young mouse deer stops needing milk. Eventually, the mouse deer leaves its mother to find its own territory. It is ready to have its own baby!

MOUSE DEER LIVE FOR ABOUT 12 YEARS IN THE WILD.

Information Station

MOUSE DEER ARE AWESOME!
LET'S LEARN EVEN MORE ABOUT THEM.

Kind of animal: Mouse deer are mammals. Mammals have fur, give birth to live young, and drink milk from their mothers as babies.

Other hoofed animals: Mouse deer are the smallest hoofed animals. Others include cows, pigs, horses, and deer.

Size: The largest mouse deer are about 33 inches (85 cm) long. That's about the size of a rabbit.

MOUSE DEER AROUND THE WORLD

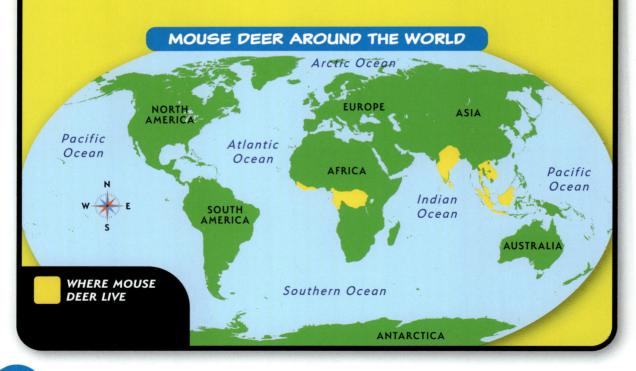

WHERE MOUSE DEER LIVE

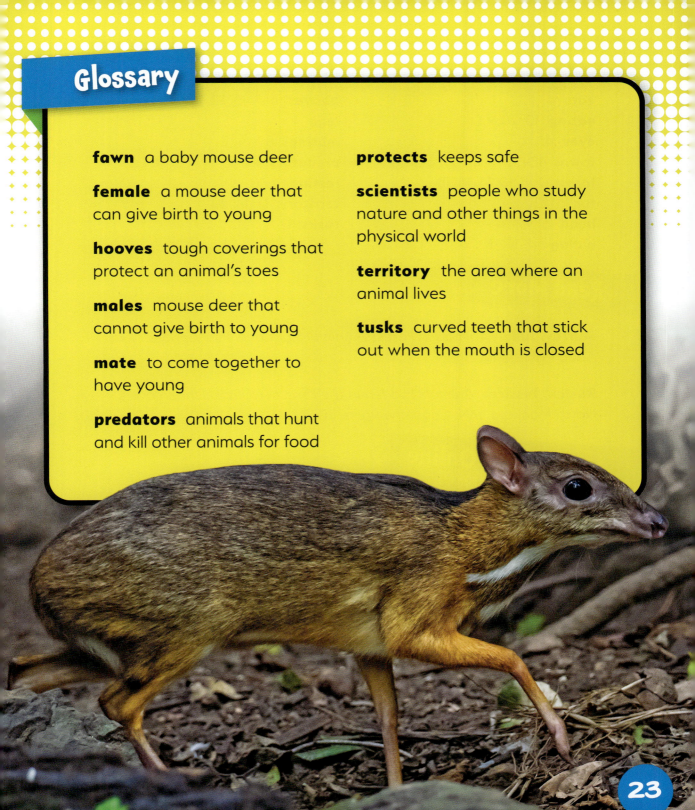

Glossary

fawn a baby mouse deer

female a mouse deer that can give birth to young

hooves tough coverings that protect an animal's toes

males mouse deer that cannot give birth to young

mate to come together to have young

predators animals that hunt and kill other animals for food

protects keeps safe

scientists people who study nature and other things in the physical world

territory the area where an animal lives

tusks curved teeth that stick out when the mouth is closed

Index

ears 4
eating 10, 20
eyes 4
fawns 18–20
forest 7–8, 10, 14, 16, 18
fur 6, 22
head 6
hiding 14–16, 18
hooves 6–7, 16, 22
legs 4
mating 18
predators 16
resting 4, 10
territory 12–14, 20
tusks 12

Read More

Murray, Julie. *Animals in Forests (Animal Habitats).* Minneapolis: Abdo Publishing, 2021.

Rusick, Jessica. *Animals Hidden in the Forest (Animals Undercover).* North Mankato, MN: Capstone Press, 2022.

Learn More Online

1. Go to **www.factsurfer.com** or scan the QR code below.
2. Enter "**Mouse Deer**" into the search box.
3. Click on the cover of this book to see a list of websites.

About the Author

Colleen Sexton is a writer and editor. She is the author of more than 100 nonfiction books for kids on topics ranging from astronauts to glaciers to sharks. She lives in Minnesota.